COLIN
THUBRON

SAMARKAND

PENGUIN BOOKS

PENGUIN BOOKS

Published by the Penguin Group. Penguin Books Ltd, 27 Wrights Lane, London
w8 5TZ, England. Penguin Books USA Inc., 375 Hudson Street, New York, New
York 10014, USA. Penguin Books Australia Ltd, Ringwood, Victoria, Australia.
Penguin Books Canada Ltd, 10 Alcorn Avenue, Toronto, Ontario, Canada M4V 3B2.
Penguin Books (NZ) Ltd, 182–190 Wairau Road, Auckland 10, New Zealand ·
Penguin Ltd, Registered Offices: Harmondsworth, Middlesex, England · These
extracts are from *The Lost Heart of Asia* by Colin Thubron, published in Penguin
Books 1995. This edition published 1996. Copyright © Colin Thubron 1994. All
rights reserved · The moral right of the author has been asserted · Typeset by Rowland
Phototypesetting Ltd, Bury St Edmunds, Suffolk. Printed in England by Clays Ltd,
St Ives plc · Except in the United States of America, this book is sold subject to
the condition that it shall not, by way of trade or otherwise, be lent, re-sold,
hired out, or otherwise circulated without the publisher's prior consent in any
form of binding or cover other than that in which it is published and without a
similar condition including this condition being imposed on the subsequent
purchaser · 10 9 8 7 6 5 4 3 2 1

'Samarkand' conjures no earthly city. It is a heart-stealing sound. Other capitals of Islam – Cairo, Damascus, Istanbul – glow with an accessible, Mediterranean magnificence. But Samarkand inhabits only the edge of geography. It rings with a landlocked strangeness, and was the seat of an empire so remote in its steppe and desert that it only touched Europe to terrify it. For centuries after it slept under obscurity, it shimmered in people's imagination. It was the fantasy of Goethe and Handel, Marlowe and Keats, yet its reality was out of reach. Even in the famous verse of the diplomat-poet Flecker, who travelled no farther east than Syria, its merchants took the golden road as if to a perilous mystery.

Over an ocean of fields and half-connected townlets, my bus made landfall at last in a nondescript depot, but I glimpsed to the east the surge and glitter of another city, circled by snow-lit mountains. For the last few miles I approached it sentimentally, on foot. I went through motley suburbs and an upthrust of flat-blocks and public buildings. A mountainous statue of Lenin was in place in a jaded square, where the slogans still bleated unread from the rooftops: 'The affairs of the world are in the hands of the people.'

From these suburban heights there opened below me a flotsam of red and grey rooftops – tin and asbestos wreckage floating on a swell of trees – studded with turquoise domes and minarets. Beyond them a long spine of snow-peaks glimmered with an unearthly radiance, and seemed to mark some ancient protection.

I went down through lorry-clogged streets. The way became sordid and ramshackle. A new harshness was in the air. An old man was praying among rosebeds on a traffic island, but had forgotten the direction of Mecca. Then, rounding a corner where buses clamoured under a flyover, I saw above me a sheaf of shattered domes and pinnacles. It started up in intermingling fawns and blues, as if a whole secret city had died within the modern one. Even in decay, it was huger than anything around it. The stubs of its entrance gate and spring of broken arches hung above the lower town as if in another ether. It was the mosque of Bibi Khanum, built by Tamerlane the Great.

I circled it in purposeful delay, past big, dim shops down avenues of plane and chestnut trees. The people looked rougher, more secular, than in Bukhara. The city was more expansive, less uniform. The wreckage of its past hovered close against its present. While Bukhara had been a warren of obscurantism, Samarkand still owned the ghostly structures of an imperial capital.

Round its old market square, the Registan, three *medresehs* ranked in near-perfect symmetry. It was almost deserted.

Once the centre of the world, it was now the centre of nothing. Even foreign sightseers had gone. Over the bare flagstones where I went, its enclosing majesty broke like a flood. In each of the three façades, a mammoth *iwan* made a gulf of shadow, and was flanked by walls tiered with shallow bays. Gate for gate, minaret for minaret, they echoed and confirmed one another. They overbore the square with an institutional solemnity, sureties of royal power and the immutability of God. To the Western eye the minarets, whose flattened tops were underhung with honeycomb decoration, conjured stout Corinthian columns supporting nothing. Earthquake had set them leaning with a crazed, plastic ease, which had teased nineteenth-century travellers into theorizing and dropping plumb-lines from them, and never quite believing it.

The tilework of their façades does not drench the eye in a faience curtain like the mosques of contemporary Persia, but splashes the brick with cool, rather cerebral designs. The colours were familiar: grape blue, turquoise, wax yellow. The buff brick interknit and sobered them. Only here and there did a ceramic frieze blaze out complete. Beneath the entrance to the fifteenth-century Ulug Beg *medreseh*, the oldest of the three, some of the panels resembled lustrous carpets, and across the *iwan* of the seventeenth-century Shir Dar a pair of heretical lions chased white does across a field of flowers.

The doors still swung over polished thresholds, but when

3

I entered the courts the only noise was birdsong. In the arcades the student cells had been locked behind their doors for decades. Some peasant women were wandering bemused over the flagstones. They followed me listlessly about. For religious students the treasures of these courts must have been the beautiful ribbons of Arabic script – always pure white against peacock blue – which overswept the arches of the *iwans* or rippled beneath their vaults. But I could not read them. Their Kufic epigraphy seemed locked away in some exquisite battle with itself.

Yet it is in these courtyards, too, that the illusion of the square evaporates. Here, suddenly, I was backstage. The grandiloquent façades, I now saw, were little more than that: an overbearing theatre set. They had no depth. Their backs were only lightly decorated, or not at all. Their duty was over. These were not shapes to be viewed in the round, but bullying stage flats which loomed over the square below in heady propaganda.

Some deadness of restoration, too, shadows all this with emptiness. The Soviets found the Registan collapsing, and began to repair it with the same diligence as they bestowed on their tsarist palaces in the west. Here a dome was reconstructed wholesale, there a minaret jacked upright; while over every dilapidated surface swept a meticulous veneer of new tiles and bricks. The interior of the central mosque, in particular, is mesmerizing. From the centre of its ceiling, in spectacular *trompe l'oeil*, a shower of gilded leaves and flowers radiates down a dark-blue sky, while the vault above the *mihrab* unfurls a fan of stalactites in coral and gold.

Only when I entered the *medreseh* of Ulug Beg did I realize what had been lost. He was the most attractive of the grandsons of Tamerlane, a scientist and astronomer who urged his pupils into secular learning. Here, in a courtyard more intimate than the others, the original decoration was still in place. It kept a subtle, broken beauty. The jigsaw of its tiles was shedding pieces everywhere, fragments easing loose from their ornamental whole, petals dropping, tendrils breaking. But for the moment it was suspended in a sweet opulence of decay. Its threatened restoration was necessary, of course; but something vital would disappear for ever. These bricks and tiles betrayed by their ageing that they belonged to the first creation: to the piety and flair of their conceivers, not to the duty of a later time. They belonged with the past. Even if the restoration were identical (and some of it is suspect) its purposes would be modern, and would leave the imagination cold.

I wondered what would happen now that Soviet rule had ended. Such mammoth reconstructions would perhaps stop, or go forward more cautiously, piecemeal. I sat for a while under the arcades, and thought ungratefully of this, while the birds were screaming in the courtyard trees, and the tiles silently, unnoticeably, were easing from their plaster and dropping into dust.

•

Inflation and instability were on everybody's lips. Everyone feared the future. In the streets the drab men and high-coloured women coalesced into crowds which consorted only asexually, men with men in shoulder-hugging embraces, women sauntering together with linked arms. Tajik-speakers, their faces yet showed every permutation between the Turanian and Iranian worlds; blunt features and eagle features, full mouths and tight.

In the government emporia, where bags of rusks, noodles and bottled fruit were stacked, almost nobody lingered. Everywhere, free markets were stirring. Yet even in the central bazaar there was no bustle, but a cautious, ambling passage in which an hour might pass in the purchase of a few carrots. It was oddly quiet. Farmers heaped their rented stalls with pomegranates, radishes, mounds of liquid cheese. But nobody had any money, and every quoted price elicited hissing and upturned noses. In the courtyard stood a blank-faced giant with a Chaplin moustache. Stripping his shirt from a massive beer gut, he lay down sacrificially under a pair of planks while a bus drove over him, then got up again, still expressionless, and circulated a money can.

He was fuller employed than many. The pavements were dark with knots of loitering youths. They were the new unemployed, and there were over a million of them in the country. They wore T-shirts inscribed 'New York' or 'Chanel'. If I were carrying my rucksack, they would eye it like psychopaths. They thought I was Estonian. 'Didn't you

6

bring anything to sell?' they demanded. They tried to work me out. 'Why are you here?' If I were seated somewhere, one of them would be sure to perch beside me like a shrike and nudge my knee or jolt my shoulder with every question, as if I had to be tormented into answering.

'Where do you come from?'

Wearily: 'Britain.'

'How is your life there? Do you get plenty to eat?'

'Yes.' I would remember, as if down a long tunnel, a race obsessed with slimming and cholesterol.

'How much do you earn?' Prod. 'How much is meat?' Prod. 'How much is a car?' Bang on shoulder. 'Will you get me a visa to Britain? How much . . . ? How much . . . ?'

Affectionately I would recall the old men in mosque court-yards, who greeted one another with a sober hand on the heart, and with only dignified inquiry. Then I would remember remorsefully that these youths, with their lost past and precarious future, their restless eyes and talk of dollars, lived in a new void, and what did I expect of them? On and on the inquisitors would nag, while I halved or quartered my income and tried to explain a world of tax and mortgage. But nothing stopped them. My prodded knee would become psychosomatically inflamed. So would my temper. And however shrivelled my earnings or qualified my answers, this dialogue always left cupidity glittering in the hard young eyes.

'They don't believe in working. They don't produce. 7

They just buy and sell things.' The stale complaint slurred on the Russian's lips. He was peering at the announcement of a dog auction to be held in the Spartak football stadium. 'And they're getting more nationalistic by the minute. But how do you leave here?' He gazed at me with the smeared eyes of the perpetually drunk, and the uninvited monologue. His fingers were ochreous with nicotine. 'I've been here all my life. My father was killed in the battles round Smolensk during the war, and this is my mother . . .' She was staring vacantly at the market. 'She's never known anywhere but here. We've nowhere to go in Russia. Her and me, it's too late for us . . . I haven't enough left.' His orange fingertips trailed over the notice. 'We'll die here.'

The old woman shuffled up beside us, her face withdrawn inside a tattered shawl. 'What are you saying?' she piped. 'What's happening?'

'We're talking about the dog auction.' She drifted away again. 'Look at her. She's already ending her days. But what do we do? We have no homeland now.'

So he was buying a dog.

Watching his creased face, I realized how deeply my concept of the Russians had changed. Suddenly everything which they had achieved here – in education, welfare, administration, however corrupt and limited – was threatening to collapse. The old, bullying propaganda – the Marxist invocations to work and unity – all at once looked like benign common sense, a plea for the future. The familiar certainties were in retreat. Russian arts – literature, music, ballet – which had once seemed the treacherous tools of colonialism, now resembled instead the rearguard of a gracious civilization, fading away before my eyes.

Even the Soviet sops to local custom had changed. Not a moment ago, it seemed, the oriental street lamps, the tulip domes above restaurants and police-posts – even the mock-Islamic latticework in the tourist hotels – had sent up a sinister smokescreen behind which a people's heart was being stolen away. Now, instead, these *kitsch* concessions seemed innocently integral to local life, like a lifted curse.

Only plastic tiles coated my restaurant, whose floor was littered with crusts and fishbones. Beggars limped from table to table. They had torn coats and split boots. They hovered above the tables as if no one was sitting there, picking at the customers' bread and drinking their tea, while the conversation went on obliviously below. As I left, one of them shambled over to my place and emptied my bowl of its mutton bones.

I went out into the ruins of the Bibi Khanum, feeling an obscure self-reproach. Even in desolation the mosque seemed to tower out of an era more fortunate than my own (but this was an illusion). Tamerlane had built it as the greatest temple in Islam. Thousands of captured artisans from Persia, Iraq and Azerbaijan had laboured to carve its marble floors, glaze its acres of tiles, erect its monster towers and the four hundred cupolas bubbling over its galleries. The emperor flailed its building forward. He considered too small the gateway completed in his absence, pulled it down wholesale, hanged its architects and began again. But the mountainous vaults and minarets which he envisioned crushed the foundations, and the walls started to fracture almost before completion. People became afraid to pray there. It towered above me in a megalomaniac reverie, raining the sky with blistered arches and severed domes. Cracks pitched and zigzagged down the walls. Tiles flaked off like skin. The gateway loomed so high that the spring of its vanished arch began eighty feet above me, and completed itself phantasmally in empty air. Gaping breaches had split the prayer-hall top to bottom, and the squinches were shedding whole bricks.

Everything – the thunderous minarets, the thirty-four doors, the outsize ablutions basin – shrank the visitor to a Lilliputian intruder, and peopled the mosque with giants. In the court's centre a megalithic lectern of grey Mongolian marble had once cradled a gargantuan Koran, but its indestructability, and perhaps its isolation in the mosque's wrecked heart, had touched it with pagan mana now, and it had become the haunt of barren women, who crouched beneath it as a charm for fertility.

As I sat nearby, three young worldlings, urban and confident in high heels and tight skirts, went giggling and nudging towards it. Their shrieks rang in the ruins. Then, separately, they dropped on all fours and crawled in and out between the lectern's nine marble legs. At first they ridiculed one another at this place where fun and superstition merged. But once unseen by their companions, creeping through the marble labyrinth, an unease descended. Covertly they touched their palms to its stone. One of them kissed it. Then they emerged, straightening their stockings, and tripped away.

Sitting by a mosque under silver poplars, Tania had inherited the gross, maternal look of Russian peasant women in poor lands. Her ginger hair dangled corkscrews round a slovenly, vegetable face, whose nose and eyes had capsized in the fatness of her cheeks. We had fallen into conversation by chance, and only as we walked together under the trees did she start to surprise me. She pointed out the grave of a Naqshbandi statesman, which stood still honoured on its mound. It was unlike a Russian to know this history, and I glanced at her in puzzlement. 'I'm married to a Muslim,' she said.

She looked so rooted in the earth of her own people that I blurted out: 'Isn't that difficult?'

'It's always difficult.' She stopped and contemplated the calligraphy on the gravestone, as if it might yield a solution. 'Muslim men are more patriarchal than us. But I don't fight with mine. He manages the money, I manage the house. But he's a wonderful cook!' She gave a hoarse, burbling laugh.

'Yes, I boss him a bit. I've stayed independent. That's why I understand my cat.'

She started to walk again, wavering fatly on her high heels. Her body conveyed a torpid, Russian strength. Her marriage was obsessing her at present, she said, because her husband was not happy. He could not relinquish his past, the memory of his first wife, who'd been a harpy. 'After she left him he sat five years alone, sulking and drinking, and he's still affected by her. He can't deny their daughters a thing.' Her face puckered in revulsion. 'They're our chief source of argument, those daughters.' She splayed out her fingers, which were stubbled in garish rings. 'And there's the cat. We argue about that. He can't accept that animals are really humans, which of course they are.' She sighed unlaughing. 'A Muslim, you see.'

I could salvage no insight from this rush of detail.

'I know other Russian women married to Tajiks and Uzbeks,' she went on, 'but each one is different. Even the prejudice. Some of my husband's family feel so violent that they can hardly bring themselves to see me. But others have been kind. There's no pattern to it.' Yet her voice was tinged with recklessness. I realized there was something I did not understand at all. 'It's hard for any Muslim's wife. But sometimes the men may start to recognize a Russian woman's intelligence. Native women are often lazy. They just sit and gossip while their children run wild. They can prepare meals, of course, but often they can't even sew.

No wonder Muslims need several wives.' She was striding beside me now, with colonial self-confidence. 'Yes, I know Tajiks who keep more than one wife – they celebrate second or even third marriages in secret with some mullah. It's hard on everyone.'

We had reached a side-gate of the mosque, whose guardian recognized her. He said quaintly: 'Guests and good men are always welcome here,' and we entered a courtyard murmuring with old men in blue turbans who leant on their sticks under the trees and dozed or hobnobbed on weathered benches. A balm of companionship filled the air, of past ways returning.

'I wanted you to see this,' Tania said. She spoke a halting Tajik with the mosque officials. They asked her where we came from, and looked pleased. Islam had always been tolerant in Central Asia, she said, without accuracy, but I knew what she meant. She did not fear religion, but politics. 'It's the politicians manipulating for their own ends – that's what frightens me. Clans. We're overrun by cliques like extended families.' Their rivalries and subterfuge crept up to the highest levels of government, I knew, and created a delicate power axis between Samarkand, Tashkent and the Fergana valley. The country's apparent unity splintered apart as you thought about it.

'But young people sometimes talk as if they had a nation now,' she said. 'They talk of being Uzbeks or Tajiks. It never used to be like that.'

'You think they feel it?'

'I don't know, I don't know.' She sounded suddenly harrowed. Some distress welled up in her whenever we touched on the future. Perhaps the old concept of a family of peoples, with Russia at its helm, was too painfully entrenched in her emotions.

We went back past a *medreseh*, and peered in. It was the largest in the city, but it seemed deserted. The student cells were locked, and pigeons massed undisturbed under the porticoes. No caretaker emerged to greet or deflect us.

Only days later did I learn the reason. According to hearsay, one of the clerics had raped a pupil. While news of this whispered through the city, the boy's relatives had assembled to tear the man to bits. But instead, after negotiations with him, they had watched while he hanged himself.

Unknowing, Tania and I walked in bewilderment through the school's silence. 'You will come and visit me soon?' she asked. Her high heels rang on the cobblestones. 'Yes. Come to us.'

The north-east suburbs break against a grassy plateau which undulates for miles. Colonies of ground squirrels stand sentinel at their burrows, and a shepherd drives his black flock over the cemetery-like ground with sharp cries. Its abrupt banks and mounds betray an earlier Samarkand decaying into the grassland. The earth seems to writhe underfoot. Sometimes it splits open on abandoned excavations. The glittering mountains stare in. Wherever the bricks rise exposed, their tamped clay has reverted to earth. The walls have become natural cliffs whose fissures had once been gates, and the ground is ripped by gullies where streets had gone, or tossed into shapeless citadels.

From the sixth century BC this ancient Samarkand, named Maracanda, was the capital of a refined Iranian people, the Sogdians, who traded along the Zerafshan valley and beyond. Alexander took the city in 329 BC, and here, in a fit of drunken hubris, transfixed his favourite general 'Black' Cleitus with a spear. But the Sogdians outlasted the fragile dynasty of Alexander's followers. Famous for their literacy and commercial cunning, it was they, perhaps, who taught the Chinese the art of glassmaking. The Romans reported that their city walls ran seven miles in circuit, and they endured here until the Arabs conquered them in AD 712. Then, little by little, they dwindled away, until Genghiz Khan wrecked Maracanda in 1220, and put the past to sleep under the loam-filled earth. Later peoples named the site from the Giant Afrasiab, a mythic king of Turan: after failing to take Maracanda by assault, they said, he had buried it in the sand.

In a museum nearby, the Sogdians falter back to life. Russian archaeologists pulled their corroded swords out of the compacted dust, their bangles, their buttons and bone clothes-pins. They seem to have worshipped early Persian gods, at a time of resurgent Buddhism. Monolithic altars 15 and carved ossuaries emerged, and some precious fragments of seventh-century fresco, in which the Sogdian king (if it is he) receives embassies from as far away as Tang-dynasty China.

They advance to meet him against a hyacinth-blue field in cavalcades of dignitaries mounted on dromedaries, horses and elephants. In airy perspective they ride harmlessly above or beneath one another, but the plaster has dropped from them in obliterating grey flakes, as if they processed through stormclouds. The lumber of elephants' feet and the prance of hooves emerge fitfully out of the decay, while a file of egrets parades inexplicably behind. The Chinese tribute-bearers carry goblets and wands in a humbled cluster of girlish eyes and close-plastered hair, and their starched dresses, embroidered with wolves' heads, seem to have hypnotized the painter. The king, meanwhile, walks forward to honour the image of his people's god. His prodigiously pearled robes woven into lozenges, his dripping ear-pendants, his soft, jewelled headdress and the necklace which dribbles nervously from his fingers, invest his kingdom with an effete strangeness. Yet his subjects' slender noses and delicate hands may have left behind their shadow in today's Tajik people.

I stumbled all afternoon over the indecipherable city, and emerged at evening by a tributary of the Zerafshan. Perched almost inaccessibly above it, under five grassy domes, was a half-forgotten tomb. An aged caretaker, slumbering nearby, opened its door in mumbled confusion, and there burgeoned before me into the gloom a monstrous mound. 'This is the tomb of the prophet Daniel,' he said. Tamerlane, he added, had brought him here from Mecca.

Like the graves of other half-legendary figures revered by the Muslims – the tombs of Noah and Nimrod in Lebanon, the sepulchre of Abel near Damascus – it was built for a titan. Local people had believed that Daniel went on growing even after death, and they lengthened his grave every year until it stretched over sixty feet. Through the decades of Russian persecution it had been silently remembered. Its walls were still black with candle flames.

I must have cut a weary figure as I trudged back along the road to Samarkand, because after a while a young Tajik in a clattering Moskvich offered me a lift. Shavgat was returning from a three-week job as a driver, and invited me home to meet his little son and old father. He was handsome in a slender, Iranian mould. Alert, candid eyes gleamed in a long head smoothed by jet-black hair. But an Islamic maleness overbore his home. He had been away three weeks, but when his young wife came to the door – a wide-eyed girl who was not quite pretty – he extended no greeting to her, only ordered her to hurry up a meal. I never saw them exchange an intimate word. Yet she was smiling and proud; for she had borne him a son.

They lived in a traditional suburb, and made me welcome. I was growing used to these compounds now, whose gates

17

clanged open on to a family courtyard where the father and his married sons each owned a stuccoed cottage, and gardens of roses and vegetables straggled in common. Inside, the walls and ceilings were painted in pale flower-patterns, and the crimson silks of newlyweds still flamed round the doors. The bride's dowry was piled up inside cupboards and cabinets in mountainous quilts – fifty or sixty of them – and pyramids of unused tea-services. Dangling above one wall, two roundels of hardened bread – a mouthful bitten out of each – had been preserved from the farewell meal for Shavgat's younger brother, who was serving as a soldier in Poland, and they would not be touched again until he returned.

Shyly Shavgat's wife carried in their infant son for my approval. A canary stuck like a toy to her shoulder. The baby clutched a papier-mâché dog sprinkled with glitter-dust. With them came Shavgat's sister-in-law, a tallow-haired Russian girl dressed in native gown and silk pantaloons. They clothed her like a submission. She was pregnant, yearning for a son of her own. But the flamboyant dress only threw into crueller relief the sallow plainness of her face. She looked slightly bitter. I longed to ask her about her situation – questions which had eluded me with Tania – but it would only have been possible alone, and soon Shavgat was parading the baby in his arms.

'Does he look like me?' he demanded. 'Does he? Does he?' I hunted in the tiny face for any resemblance, but it only reflected – as in some simplified cartoon – the wide gaze and cusped mouth of the mother. She might have produced him alone, by parthenogenesis. 'Tell me. Does he look like me?'

But the moment was saved by Shavgat's father, a gross, wily-faced peasant. He seized his grandson – the family obsession – and dandled him ferociously on his shoulder, while the child screamed and plucked at his Brezhnev eyebrows. The old man sobered only to pour scorn on modern times. 'Everything's terrible now. In Rashidov's day the shops were full and everything was cheap!' He flung his arm across their supper table. 'This would have been covered then. Covered! Meat was only three roubles a kilo, and now it's ninety. And vodka, three roubles a bottle. Now it's a hundred!'

Their luxuries in these bare rooms were few and cherished. A cageful of canaries fluttered and sang; a little stock of Marlboro cigarettes collected in a niche; and before sleep Shavgat rubbed handcream delicately into his palms, as if it were magic. We slept under quilts along the floor, he with his hands folded carefully over his stomach, while his wife went into the bedroom, her hair released down her back. The canaries fidgeted to a standstill, then never stirred all night, as if stuffed.

In the silence I asked about the photograph of a woman hung in honour on the wall above us. A weak bulb dangling over the door lit up an unreadable sepia face. 'That's my mother,' Shavgat said. 'She and my father have been 19 separated many years.' His voice fell away. 'Yes, it's unusual with us Tajiks. But she's a fine woman.' He said nothing more, except that she was living in Chimkent – a beautiful town, where he sometimes visited her – and that she had never married again.

For two thousand years Central Asia was the womb of terror, where an implacable queue of barbarian races waited to impel one another into history. Whatever spurred their grim waves – the deepening erosion of their pasturelands or their seasons of fleeting unity – they bore the same stamp of phantom mobility and mercilessness.

Two and a half millennia ago the shadowy Scythians of Herodotus – Aryan savages whose country was the horse – simmered just beyond the reach of civilization, like a ghastly protoplasm of all that was to come. Then the Huns flooded over the shattered Roman Empire in a ravening swarm – fetid men clothed in whatever they had slaughtered, even the sewn skins of fieldmice – and they did not stop until they had reached Orleans, and their rude king Attila had died in unseasonable bridebed, and their kingdom flew to pieces. But the Avars followed them – long-haired centaurs who rocked Constantinople and were eventually obliterated by Charlemagne at the dawn of the ninth century. Soon afterwards an enfeebled Byzantium let in the Magyars, and the fearsome Pechenegs rushed in after – Turanian peoples, all of them, who evaporated at last in the gloomy European forests, or settled to become Christian on the Great Hungarian Plain.

Then, at the start of the thirteenth century, as Christian Europe ripened and Islamic Asia flourished, the dread steppeland unleashed its last holocaust in the Mongols. This was not the random flood of popular imagination, but the assault of a disciplined war machine perfected by the genius of Genghiz Khan. Unpredictable as a dust-storm, its atrocious cavalry – neckless warriors with dangling moustaches – could advance at seventy miles a day, enduring any hardship. Only their stench, it was said, gave warning of their coming. In extremes, they drank from the jugulars of their horses and ate the flesh of wolves or humans. Yet they were armoured in habergeons of iron or laminated leather scales, and they could fire their steel-tipped arrows with magic accuracy over more than two hundred yards at full gallop. Consummate tacticians and scouts, they soon carried in their wake siege-engines and flame-throwers, and around their nucleus of ethnic Mongols rode a formidable mass of Turkic auxiliaries.

By Genghiz Khan's death their empire unfurled from Poland to the China Sea. Within a few years his sons and grandsons came within sight of Vienna, laid waste Burma and Korea, and sailed, disastrously, for Japan. Meanwhile, in their Central Asian heartland, the *Pax mongolica* was instilling administrative discipline, commercial recovery, and a frightened peace.

Tamerlane, the Earth-shaker, was the last, and perhaps most awesome, of these world predators. Born in 1336 fifty miles south of Samarkand, he was the son of a petty chief in a settled Mongol clan. He acquired the name 'Timur-i-Leng' or 'Timur the Lame' after arrows maimed his right leg and arm, and passed as Tamerlane into the fearful imagination of the West. By his early thirties, after years of fighting over the splintered heritage of Genghiz Khan, he had become lord of Mavarannah, the 'Land beyond the River', with his capital at Samarkand, and had turned his cold eyes to the conquest of the world.

From the accounts that are left of him, he emerges not only as the culmination of his pitiless forerunners, but as the distant ancestor of the art-loving Moghuls of India. Over the terrified servants and awed ambassadors at his court, his eyes seemed to burn without brilliance, and never winced with either humour or sadness. But a passion for practical truth fed his unlettered intelligence. He planned his campaigns in scrupulous detail, and unlike Genghiz Khan he led them in person. He clothed his every move with the sanction of the Islamic faith, but astrology and omens, shamanism and public prayers, were all invoked to serve his needs. An angel, it was rumoured, told him men's hidden thoughts. Yet he assaulted Muslims as violently as he did Christians and Hindus. Perhaps he confused himself with God.

22   No flicker of compassion marred his progress. His

butchery surpassed that of any before him. The towers and pyramids of skulls he left behind – 90,000 in the ruins of Baghdad alone – were calculated warnings. After over-running Persia and despoiling the Caucasus, he hacked back the remnants of the Golden Horde to Moscow, then launched a precipitate attack on India, winching his horses over the snowbound ravines of the Hindu Kush, where 20,000 Mongols froze to death. On the Ganges plain before Delhi, the Indian sultan's squadrons of mailed elephants, their tusks lashed with poisoned blades, sent a momentary tremor through the Mongol ranks; but the great beasts were routed, and the city and all its inhabitants levelled with the earth. A year later the Mongols were wending back over the mountains, leading 10,000 pack-mules sagging with gold and jewels. They left behind a land which would not recover for a century, and 5 million Indian dead.

Now Tamerlane turned his attention west again. Baghdad, Aleppo, Damascus fell. In 1402, on the field of Ankara, at the summit of his power, he decimated the army of the Ottoman sultan Beyazid, and inadvertently delayed the fall of Constantinople by another half century.

Between these monotonous acts of devastation, the conqueror returned to the Samarkand he cherished. At his direction a procession of captured scholars, theologians, musicians and craftsmen arrived in the capital with their books and tools and families – so many that they were forced to inhabit caves and orchards in the suburbs. Under their hands the mud city bloomed into faience life. Architects, painters and calligraphers from Persia; Syrian silk-weavers, armourers and glass-blowers; Indian jewellers and workers in stucco and metal; gunsmiths and artillery engineers from Asia Minor: all laboured to raise titanic mosques and academies, arsenals, libraries, vaulted and fountained bazaars, even an observatory and a menagerie. The captured elephants lugged into place the marble of Tabriz and the Caucasus, while rival emirs – sometimes Tamerlane himself – drove on the work with the parvenu impatience of shepherd-princes. The whole city, it seems, was to be an act of imperial power. Villages were built around it named Cairo, Baghdad, Shiraz or Damascus (a ghostly Paris survives) in token of their insignificance. It was the 'Mirror of the World', and the premier city of Asia.

Tamerlane himself confounds simple assessment. He kept a private art collection, whose exquisitely illuminated manuscripts he loved but could not read. His speech, it seems, was puritan in its decorum. He was an ingenious and addicted chess-player, who elaborated the game by doubling its pieces – with two giraffes, two war-engines, a vizier and others – over a board of 110 squares. A craving for knowledge plunged him into hard, questing debates with scholars and scientists, whom he took with him even on campaign, and his quick grasp and powerful memory gave him a working knowledge of history, medicine, mathematics and astronomy.

Yet at heart he was a nomad. He moved between summer

and winter pastures with his whole court and horde. Even at Samarkand he usually pavilioned in the outskirts, or in one of the sixteen gardens he spread round the city: watered parks with ringing names. Each garden was different. In one stood a porcelain Chinese palace; another glowed with the saga of his reign in lifelike frescoes, all long vanished; yet another was so vast that when a workman lost his horse there it grazed unfound for six months.

In such playgrounds were held the *fêtes champêtres* witnessed by the Castilian envoy Ruy Gonzalez de Clavijo. At the wedding of six royal princes (including the eleven-year-old Ulug Beg) he described how 20,000 tents covered the meadows near Samarkand for a month. The central pavilion alone accommodated 10,000 guests. Its forty-foot mountain of silk cascaded from a dome woven with eagles, billowed down above 500 vermilion guy-ropes, then reared up again to turrets crested with silk battlements. In the banqueting tents a gluttonous feasting and drinking took hold. Enormous leather platters were dragged in, heaped with sheep's heads, horse croupes and tripe in balls the size of a man's fist. After one such feast came a ceremonial presentation of gifts, and Clavijo writes with pride that his Spanish tapestries were outshone only by the Egyptian delegation's presentation of nine ostriches and a giraffe. The city's guilds threw themselves into sumptuous displays of ingenuity. The linen-weavers constructed an armoured horseman in pure linen, 'even to the nails and eyelids', while the cotton-workers erected a hundred-foot minaret in flax, crowned by a cotton stork. The butchers dressed up animals as humans; the furriers disguised humans as wild beasts.

But among the tents, in black warning, there dangled from gallows the bodies of the mayor of Samarkand and the emirs who had bungled the gateway of the Bibi Khanum mosque, with the corpses of merchants who had overpriced their wares.

At last, as the autumn nights darkened towards winter, Tamerlane ordered the tents rolled up and turned his ageing eyes towards the richest quarry remaining: China. With an army a quarter of a million strong, he marched north towards the Jaxartes valley, planning to strike east with the first hint of spring. But the winter was the coldest in memory. The rivers froze and blizzards howled out of Siberia. Men, horses, camels, elephants struggled through deepening drifts. 'Seared by the cold,' wrote Tamerlane's Arab biographer, 'men's noses and ears fell off. They froze to death as they rode . . . Yet Tamerlane cared not for their dying, nor grieved for those who had fallen.'

Soon after they reached their base camp, the emperor fell into a shivering sickness. Wine laced with spices and hot drugs had no effect, so his doctors laid icepacks on his chest and head, until he coughed up blood. Then they despaired. 'We know of no cure for death,' they said. Towards nightfall, while a thunderstorm raged outside, Tamerlane called together his family and emirs, and appointed his successor.

Then to the sound of imams' chanting in the neighbouring room, and the crashing of the tempest, the monster died.

He was buried in Samarkand in the mausoleum which he had prepared for his favourite grandson, dead of wounds two years before. The college and hospice which once enclosed it have been effaced by earthquake, and it rises alone among alleys intimate with mulberry trees, whose fruit crunched underfoot at my approach. Its courtyard gate stood up in fragile solitude. Ruins made a phantom geometry inside. Among them a marble platform, carved with flower tendrils, had been the coronation stone of the emirs of Bukhara.

But beyond this, above a façade to which broken minarets and a few tiles stuck, a ribbed dome swelled like the calyx of an unearthly flower. Chance had stripped bare everything around it, so that it floated pure above a high drum, on which 'God is Immortal' blazed in white Kufic letters as tall as a man. Above this, a belt of recessed corbels lifted the dome through its faint but seductive swelling towards the elliptic. It was a dome peculiar to Central Asia, grooved like a cantaloup melon. Up each of its faience ribs, against an aquamarine field, went diamond lozenges in lapis blue. I had seen it in picture books as a child, redolent of desert farness.

I crossed the courtyard and found myself in a bare passageway. At its end, on either side of a low door, hung a broken Kufic frieze, huge, as if displaced from somewhere else. 'This is the resting place of the Illustrious and Merciful Monarch, the Magnificent Sultan, the most Mighty 27

Warrior, Emir Timur Kurgan, Conqueror of all the Earth'
ran the original inscription; but it had gone.

I peered through the doors and into the chamber. The
latticed windows let in diffused sunbeams. High above me,
across the whole summit of the dome, fanned a net of gilded
stucco, which twined upon itself in mathematic delicacy.
It dropped its golden creepers over the enormous spandrels,
bays and pendentives, and shed a soft blaze of light on to
everything below. Beneath it the walls were coated in alabaster – hexagonal tiles, still translucent – and circled by a jasper
frieze carved with the deeds and genealogy of the emperor.
Beneath this again, within the low balustrade at my feet, the
cenotaphs of his family lay side by side in rectangular blocks
of marble and alabaster. And at the centre, stark among their
pallor, the grave of Tamerlane shone in a monolith of near-
black jade. It was disconcertingly beautiful: the largest block
of jade in the world. Its edges were lightly inscribed. A vertical
split showed where Persian soldiers (it is thought) had hacked
at it two and half centuries before.

I stayed here a long time, at once moved and unsettled.
A man entered and prayed for a while, then went away.
The cries of children sounded faintly outside. Under the
decorated brilliance of the cupola, the simplicity of these
gravestones was dignified and rather terrible: a recogni-
tion of the littleness even of this man, and the passage
of time. Beside him lay his gentle son Shah Rukh; at his
head, his minister; under a bay, his sheikh. His grand-

son Ulug Beg was at his feet. Others were gathered round.

At last the young caretaker, pleased by my interest, ushered me out of the chamber and led me round the back of the mausoleum. He unlocked a tiny carved door. 'Here is the real grave,' he said.

I descended a steep, ramped passage beneath the building. In the blackness I sensed the sweep of vaults low overhead. Somewhere behind me, the man turned a switch, and a bare bulb made a pool of dimness in the crypt. Each cenotaph in the chamber above was mirrored in this darkness by a flat gravestone. They lay secret in their dust and silence. The air was dry and old. I knelt by the emperor's graveslab and touched it. Beneath, wrapped in linen embalmed in camphor and musk, his shrunken body had been laid in an ebony coffin. I could not imagine it. The living man was too vivid in my mind. For a year after his interment, it was said, people heard him howling from the earth.

In the dull light I saw that every inch of the marble slab seethed with carved Arabic, as if even the words were waging a battle across his stone. They traced his ancestry back through Genghiz Khan (a claim he never made in life) to the legendary virgin Alangoa, ravished by a moonbeam, and at last to Adam.

The stone was split clean across in two places; but when Soviet archaeologists opened it in 1941 they found undisturbed the skeleton of a powerful man, lame on his right side. Fragments of muscle and skin still clung to him, and 29 scraps of a russet moustache and beard. An untraceable story warned that if Tamerlane's grave was violated, disaster would follow, and a few hours later news arrived that Hitler had invaded Russia.

But the investigations went on, and from the emperor's skull the Soviet scientist Gerasimov painstakingly reconstructed a bronze portrait-head, before sealing Tamerlane back in the tomb. Under the sculptor's hands there emerged a face of hardened power, compassionless, bitter and subtle. Perhaps some Slavic prejudice heightened the epicanthic cruelty of the eyes; perhaps not. A hint of the emperor's youthful truculence tinges the full lips, but that is all. Cord-like ligaments scoop the cheeks into harrowed triangles. Ancient muscles knot the cheeks, and a heraldic flexion of the brows seems to signal the sack of a city.

'He was a hero,' said a voice behind me. I jumped. The caretaker had entered noiselessly and was looking down at the tumult of calligraphy on the slab. 'What a history!'

'Perhaps he should have done less,' I said.

'Less? No. Timur turned us into one country.' He seemed lighthearted, but a reticent evangelism tinged him. 'Yes, he was cruel, I know. People come to this grave from Iran and Afghanistan and they hate him. They say, "He destroyed our land, he enslaved us!" And of course it's true. He smashed Isfahan and Baghdad.' He smiled charmingly. 'He was ruthless.'

30   I said: 'Ulug Beg might be a better hero for your nation.'

My eyes drifted affectionately over his graveslab. It was richly inscribed too.

The caretaker laughed. The sound made a soft insult in the silence. 'He was only a teacher.' He squatted beside me above the stones. 'But Timur was world-class! If I was an Iranian, I'd hate him too!' He was laughing at himself a little; after all, it was long ago. 'But Timur was not a savage. He knew about Alexander of Macedon, and the slave leader Spartacus and . . .'

'Spartacus?' This was a Soviet cult leftover. 'Did he?'

'. . . and he'd read the great Persian poet Firdausi, who claimed that the Iranians were natural rulers and the Turks were natural slaves.' He cocked his head at the gravestone, as if trying to read that tremendous obituary. 'Our two worlds have always been at war. And when Timur overran Persia and came to Firdausi's tomb he shouted: "Stand up! Look at me! A Turk in the heart of your empire! You said we were slaves, but look now!"'

His words rang in the dark. We both fancied, I think, that the dead were listening. He glowed with vicarious triumph. Tamerlane for him was the unifier and recreator of his notional fatherland, of the Pan-Turkic dream. He said: 'The Persians were here once, you see. You've been to Afrasiab? You've seen those Sogdian paintings, Persian things? They were our conquerors.'

'Those paintings are extraordinary . . .'

'So Timur avenged us. He created a Turkish empire!'

His voice had whetted into a funeral oration. He had the northerner's scorn for the soft, dark people of the south. 'He's our hero.'

I said: 'But he was a Mongol.'

'No, Timur was not a Mongol, he was a Turk.'

I stayed silent. Everyone was claiming Tamerlane now. Uzbeks and even Tajiks whom I met would debonairly enrol him in their nations. In fact Tamerlane had been a pure Mongol of the Barlas clan, infected by Turkic customs. But this pedantry could not staunch the caretaker's sense of ownership or belonging.

'I may be an Uzbek,' he said, 'but above all I am a Turk. Most people have forgotten their tribes now, but I know my father was a Kungrat, my mother a Mangit – these are Turkic tribes.'

'They're Uzbek tribes too.'

'But you can't *feel* Uzbek.' He was losing the infant Uzbek nation in a Turkic sea. 'Look at our ancestors! We have Navoi, we have Mirkhwand, we have . . .' His last spilt into the unknown for me. In fact his people were ethnically too complex to shelter under any name. Even his Turkic umbrella was full of Persian holes. The hero of Uzbek literature, the fifteenth-century Timurid poet Navoi, had written of Uzbeks only to disparage them. Yet his name and image were as ubiquitous in Uzbekistan as Makhtumkuli's in Turkmenistan. Young in their state, Uzbeks and Tajiks were suddenly annexing poets or scientists out of the past, steeping their nation in the magic of great men. The Tajiks were even appropriating Saadi and Omar Khayyám, any Persian at all. To challenge such claims was to wander an ethnic labyrinth until the concept of a country became meaningless.

The caretaker got to his feet, still reeling off names, and we started to return up the passageway. '. . . And we have Timur!'

He switched off the sad bulb and locked the narrow door behind us. In the sanity of daylight he relented a little. 'Well,' he said, 'occasionally somebody *does* feel quite strongly "I'm an Uzbek"' – he feebly thumped his chest – 'but you don't hear it much.'

We walked round the mausoleum in the sun. Some ease and lightness had returned to us. Uzbek independence had freed him into pride, he said, instead of condemning him to some Slavic sub-species. 'Of course I'm pleased by it. Everyone I know is pleased. You've found some not? Well, those are the uneducated.' He spoke the word without regret. 'Some people don't know what to feel. They can't see beyond their faces. They just know that things are bad now. But I'm thinking of my children, and the world they'll grow into. I want it to be their own.'

We stopped at the mouth of a shaft descending through grilles beneath the sanctuary. When I set my eye to it, I descried grey rectangles suspended far down in the blackness, and realized that I was gazing into the crypt. It was a vent for whispered prayers. I straightened and moved away, shaking off the notion that some dreadful authority lingered in those shreds of gristle and calcium under the stone.

The man went on eagerly: 'How can anyone regret the Soviet Union falling to bits? They bled us. In the old days they gave us five kopeks for a kilo of cotton. Just *five kopeks*. One factory in Russia used to make two shirts out of a kilo and sell them for *forty roubles* each. Moscow said we were partners, but what kind of partnership is that?' He clasped my hand in illustration. 'Partnership should mean friendship, shouldn't it?' We had circled the building now, and the handclasp turned into farewell. As I walked back across the courtyard, his shouted optimisms followed me to the gate. 'Enjoy our country! Everything will get better!'

Above him the great dome made a lonely tumour above the ogre-king.

I wandered one Sunday morning among suburbs blooming with chestnut trees, where birds sang in the unaccustomed stillness. All around clustered those brick cottages which seem to cover the old Soviet empire in petrified log huts. It might have been a suburb of Novgorod or Oryol. But nobody was about. In front of me a brick cathedral thrust up its gaudy spire where the bells had hung silent for seventy years. In the aftermath of *perestroika* a few women in bedsocks and slippers were begging near the entrance, and now the belfry sent up a hesitant, rusty clanking.

Inside, where a congregation of a thousand might have worshipped, some eighty faithful stood in broken ranks. Old women cowled in headscarves, with a few children and lanky young men, they belonged in the Belorussian fields, not here in the heart of Asia. But they kissed and embraced each other as they ambled among the icons, and slowly a feel of family security brewed up. This, after all, was their trans-posed homeland: the mystical body of Christ, where the massed contingents of saints, Church fathers and attendant angels – the whole hierarchy of Orthodox holiness – mounted the walls and pillars in arcs of candle flame. Across the iconostasis they unfurled their white wings and fingered blessings. St Basil the Great, St Nicholas, St Theodore, St George on his white charger – their Slavic eyes and brandished swords and books encircled the faithful with the comfort of an immemorial truth.

But my heart sank. The people looked beleaguered. Their singing quavered and whined in the void. A few acolytes in pale violet drifted back and forth like disconsolate angels, and in the balcony a little choir set up a shrill, heartbreaking chant, whose verses lifted and died away like an old, repeated grief. Beneath them, where a verse should have come, the people seemed to let out a deep, collective sigh. They had survived the blows of Communism only to face nationalism and Islam, and they seemed now as remote to this land as the time when their saints were flesh, and God was in the world.

Then the doors of the iconostasis burst open on a huge, gold-robed priest, who raised his arms in prayer. Where Western prelates beseech God with an alto sanctimoniousness, Russia turns out these booming giants who seem to understudy Him. The whole church at once filled up with a Chaliapin thunder, and the liturgy went forward in a deafening, homely pomp. As the incense spurted from the thurible, each sweep of the priest's arm could have felled a tree. The coals grated and the sweet smoke rose. A domestic balm descended on the worshippers. All was familiar, theirs, right. From time to time one of the old women would trundle away to kiss a saint or calm a baby or top up an oil lamp. But she would return to cross herself again and again, while the groves of candles blossomed beneath favourite icons.

Meanwhile the processions of the gold-embossed Gospel and the elevated Sacrament, swollen on the voice of the priest, brought on a fresh flurry of self-blessings, and at last the silver Eucharist spoon, dipped into the chalice beneath a scarlet napkin, administered the body and blood of Christ like a wholesome medicine. Even I felt a sense of remission. For this hour, at least, all seemed well among the dwindling faithful, as they and the priest and the dim-lit saints watched and nurtured one another into the unknown future.

On the north-east outskirts of the city a sunken trajectory of domes and gates traces a funerary way up Maracanda's ruined ramparts. In this secret glade, through the late fourteenth century, the women and warriors of Tamerlane were laid in sepulchres whose precious tiles, carried on camelback from Persia, were fitted round the tomb façades in a cool splendour.

In early morning, before any tour groups arrive, you may walk up this avenue undisturbed, while the dawn leaks a thin light over its walls. At its foot a mullah waits in a newly working mosque; but beyond, the screams of swallows ricochet among the domes, and the way ascends over hexagonal flagstones between the mausoleums. Their cupolas donot swell and bloom, but complete their graves modestly, like a wardrobe of antique hats. A few plane trees lean over the path. Here and there a building has vanished, leaving an anonymous hump.

Then the first pilgrims appear. Peasant women mostly, gleaming in gold-splintered scarves and iridescent leggings, and trailing picnic bags, they toil up to the entombed saint who casts over this place a halo of miracle. But on the way they squat inside the chambers where the half pagan Mongol aristocracy lies, and smooth their palms over the stones, and murmur, 'Allah, Allah.' Methuselahs with sticks and flaking beards, and dowagers whose shawls pile their heads like the wimples of medieval burghers, they ease themselves upwards in an aura of pious holiday.

Half way along, the ascent bends through an overhanging gateway, and there opens up a zone of disciplined brilliance. The acres of lightly patterned brick which covered contemporary mosques contract to an aisle of private piety and grief. To either side its walls and high entranceways are clothed in waterfalls of pure faience. Sometimes the façades converge across the way with barely twelve feet between them, echoing one another with the lustrous intimacy of miniatures. Two sisters of Tamerlane are buried here, and a young wife, Tuman, all of whom predeceased him. Inside, the chambers are nearly bare. Here and there a smashed tile sticks to a grave or a shadow of fresco lingers, but the cenotaphs are simple cubes and rectangles, mostly uninscribed. It is the entranceways which give voice to the distinction, and perhaps the belovedness, of the dead. They are tiled vertically by eight or ten different friezes in turquoise and gentian-blue, powdered with stars, wheels, flowers: a whole lexicon of motifs. They hang there in ravishing detail. Sometimes white inscriptions twine them. Occasionally a touch of oxblood or pale green intrudes. Many panels are raised in deep relief, as if wrapped in a veil of loose knitting, so the sun glitters over them unpenetrating. They are an aesthete's paradise.

But pilgrims steer for the avenue's end and the tomb of the legendary Kussam ibn-Abbas, cousin of the Prophet, who carried Islam to Samarkand, it is said, and was martyred here in the seventh century. 'Those who were killed on the way of Allah are not to be considered dead; indeed, they are alive,' runs the *aya* on his grave, and it is perhaps from this that the necropolis takes its name of Shakhi-Zinda, 'the Shrine of the Living King'. As late as the 1920s, before Stalin stifled religion, its underground cells were full of devotees fasting and contemplating in enforced silence for forty days at a time. The martyr, they said, lingered here unseen 'in the living flesh', waiting to expel the Russians. Beyond the shrine, all along the sunlit heights of the vanished ramparts, thousands of graves still spread within the sacred force-field of his tomb.

A pair of deep-carved walnut doors lurches open on its antechamber. Dust-filled beams of light hang in the dark. Glimpsed through its grille, the porcelain grave is delicate and small. It unfurls in four jewelled tiers upon the bare floor.

'It was the fire-worshippers who killed him. Persians, you know. They cut off his head.' The burly, soft-faced man who dispensed prayers here touched his neck with a karate chop. 'But then what happened? The saint didn't die, no. He picked up his head and jumped with it into a well!' He tucked an aerial head under his arm, like a Tudor ghost. 'And there he waits to return, in the Garden of Paradise.'

Crouched along the walls beside us, ranks of village women let out bleating hymns, their scarves dropped over their faces, their legs doubled under them, their shoes off.

Sometimes they turned their furrowed hands upwards while old men led them in half-sung prayer. A bevy of town girls came in and squatted opposite self-consciously. They were necklaced in seed-pearls over their high-ruffed dresses, and their hair drawn tight under nacreous clasps in the style of the day. They fell silent almost at once, listening to the unfamiliar words. They seemed to be sucking nourishment back out of their past, learning from these ancient peasants who they were, or who they might yet be.

From time to time the burly man went out to pray with other pilgrims in his cell – a converted tomb – where I would hear him chanting in a plangent, musical voice before he returned to sit in the sun. The whole sanctuary was resurrecting now, he said. Its mosque, closed down since Khrushchev's day, was open again, and the pilgrims returning.

And what of the saint, I asked? Had there been miracles?

He could not answer for others, he said. 'But I myself . . . I used to have high blood pressure. It got up into my eyes somehow, and into my kidneys. I thought I might not have long to live, and the doctors couldn't do a thing. So I came here to clean the dust round the saint's tomb.' He gazed at the walnut doors with rested eyes. 'And now I'm well again.'

Then a younger man sat down beside us. I saw, beneath the cap of a *medreseh* student, a white, possessed face. He wanted to know what we had been saying. The burly man went silent. Under the student's hot, arid stare our conversation spluttered up again, then died.

A *medreseh* had opened recently in Samarkand, he said coldly, and he was there. I remembered it, of course, and the rape and the mullah's suicide, but said nothing. 'The top graduates,' he went on, 'will complete their studies for a few months in Saudi Arabia or Iran or Pakistan.'

I tried hopefully: 'Doesn't your Islam differ a little from theirs?'

He hooked his forefingers into a knot of indissoluble union. 'We are all one. The Koran is one. Our faith is one.'

I sat there a long time, touched with alarm, before he went away, irritated by my questions. The burly man remained seated in silence beside me, relaxed in the sunlight. Now the Russians had gone, I asked, what enemy was left for the Living King to expel? Couldn't he rest?

'I don't know. You'd have to ask others things like that. But the saint expels the sorrow in people. That's why they come here.' An old woman was kissing the door jambs in front of us. 'And eventually he will return.'

'You believe that?'

'Yes, I believe it. He'll return at the end of the light.' A millennial fatalism overtook him. 'Perhaps if we live long enough, we'll see it.'

I went back down the funerary way, wondering about the nature of its dead. (Who, for instance, had been the niece of Tamerlane laid under a dome decorated pathetically with faience tears?) As I passed the grave of the astronomer Kazyade, teacher and friend of Ulug Beg, my thoughts 41 turned to heresy and science, and a confused train of history flooded in.

All through the fifteenth century Central Asia was filled by the quarrels and luxuries of the Timurid princes, successors of Tamerlane, with their poetry and miniatures (and weakness for wine and catamites). Hedonism and science ran free. Tamerlane's son Shah Rukh reigned – a mighty prince – from Herat in Afghanistan, where years before I had seen his wife's college toppling in ruin, while their own son Ulug Beg governed as viceroy and then sultan in Samarkand. A century later a great-great-great-grandson of the emperor, Babur, ruled here in brief happiness before fleeing the Uzbek invaders south, and left behind him an autobiography of entrancing humanity. It was he, years later, who founded the Moghul empire in India, and carried into its rice deltas the vigour and epicurism of Central Asia, whose bulbous domes were to fruit in the Taj Mahal. Here the schizophrenic spirit of Tamerlane survived (or so I fancied) among the imperial chess-players and refined Moghul gardens, and lingered too in sudden, often intimate acts of cruelty – that terrible divorce of aestheticism from compassion which was to trouble all his descendants.

In Samarkand meanwhile, the empire of the dead conqueror was disintegrating. Its economy was too shallow to support it. The city workshops still produced their rich cloths and metal, and the finest paper in the world – a skill taught here by the Chinese seven centuries before – but the

Silk Road was dying. Tamerlane's wider conquests, which settled no government in their wake, were now revealed only as the megalomaniac raids of a brilliant predator.

Ulug Beg, his grandson, ruled with a different glory. In the 100-foot observatory which he built on a hill outside Samarkand, frescoed with embodiments of the celestial spheres, a caucus of astronomers and mathematicians fussed over azimuths and planispheres, traced the precession of the equinoxes and determined the ecliptic. Here he discovered two hundred unknown stars, and recalculated the stellar year to within a few seconds of that computed by modern electronics. But the pietists, of course, hated him, and in 1449 he was killed by reactionaries led by his own son. His observatory was damned 'the cemetery of the forty evil spirits', and levelled with the ground.

In 1908 a Russian schoolmaster, Vladimir Vyatkin, after calculating where the observatory must have stood, dug down and hit the arc of what appeared to be a primitive escalator. Now sheltered under a modern vault, its twin marble parapets swoop side by side through the excavated earth. Meticulously jointed and calibrated, they are the section of a titanic 180-foot quadrant along whose rails ran the astrolabe by which Ulug Beg bearded God and identified the heavens.

The Victory Day celebrations were muted that year. For the first time, there was no parade. Down the memorial avenue red flags still mingled with the national colours, and groups of Russian and Tajik veterans were hobbling separately, their chests ablaze with medals, towards the temple which sheltered the eternal flame. But a mournfulness of anticlimax hung about them. The ragged line of police had nothing to supervise. On either side, Second World War tanks and anti-aircraft guns stood on their plinths like relics of prehistory, and martial music sobbed from the loudspeakers. Inside the red-stoned cube of the temple, lilies, peonies, carnations and irises were banked around the sacred fire. 'Nobody must forget,' raged the slogans. But young Tajiks and Uzbeks with their families were strolling about on holiday, and glanced curiously at the shuffling mourners, who looked suddenly redundant as if – in this empire of long memories – the war were at last receding.

'I was at Potsdam and Berlin,' confided one man. His lapels dripped with medals. 'Look.' He bowed his head to me. Under its powder of hair the skull was dented by a cavity empurpled with veins. I would not have thought anybody could survive such a wound. 'I got that a week before the war's end!'

'I'm amazed you're still alive!'

'Alive? I've marched every year in the parade.'

'I missed it.'

'Well, there wasn't one. There's only this now.' He jerked his chin at the silent veterans trudging about the flowers. He looked belligerent. 'It's because of that Gorbachev and everything he did . . .' He scanned me with filmy eyes. 'Were you in the war?'

'No.' I wondered how old I was looking. 'But my father fought in North Africa and Italy.'

'North Africa . . . Italy . . .' The words fell experimentally from him. After their appalling sacrifice, Russians often forget that anyone but they confronted Germany. But suddenly he squeezed my arm in a brotherhood which overleapt the continents, and kissed my cheeks, so that I was moved by a vicarious pride, and I wished my father there.

'Next year, I tell you,' he said, as if to comfort me, 'there'll be a parade again.' He opened his arms like a boasting angler. 'A *huge* parade!'

I wandered away into the memorial gardens. Tajik and Uzbek veterans were walking there too, and an old woman in full decorations was posing for her photograph. In their remembered war they converged – native and Russian together – at a point where time had superseded race. I went down glades lined with the busts of Heroes of the Soviet Union.

'Look at them,' one of the Uzbeks said. 'The heroes are still there, but the Soviet Union's gone!' A delta of smile-lines flowed from his mouth and eyes, but he was not happy. He had the face of a wizened monkey. 'I tell you as an old man, as a veteran of the Great Patriotic War, that it's a bad thing. Absolutely a bad thing.'

'You don't want independence?'

'No! Everything's got worse. And it'll go on getting worse and worse.'

I stared at him, still touched by a vague wonder at the gap where nationalism might have been. A pair of policemen shambled by, their hats tilted back on their heads.

'Only young people are glad,' he said disgustedly, 'because they don't have to do any work. Look at those police! They just play-act and take bribes.' He bent his arm in a mock salute. 'Nobody works any more.'

This, I knew, was more than the perennial complaint of the old against the young, the lament for uninherited beliefs. A gulf of unshared experience gaped between the generations. The world was slipping away from him. 'And you wait,' he said, as we circled back to the eternal flame. 'In a minute hooligans will come and steal the flowers.'

I loitered until noon while the crowds thinned. The soulful music throbbed and tramped in the loudspeakers overhead, as if the dead were on the march again, accusing.

South from Samarkand a broad road ran fifty miles to Shakhrisabz, over an outlying finger of the Pamir. Beyond foothills rose a wraith-like curtain of mountains whose pelmet was lost in cloud. As my crammed taxi started to climb, the crags surged unsteadily about us in the mist. Everything paled, until the web of our splintered windscreen overlay only a watercolour softness beyond. Sometimes the road reverted to a cracked causeway unchanged since Soviet tanks moved down it to Afghanistan in 1979. All around, the mountain-scarps hung in diseased-looking palisades of flaking rock. Then we topped the pass and stared down through haze. A sandy fox watched us from the mossed rocks. Nothing else stirred. Half an hour later we had arrived in Shakhrisabz.

It was a cool, harmonious town. To either side, the porcelain mountains herded it into its lush valley, and hung the sky with disembodied snow. The tea-houses along its main street were leisurely with old men, and the parks soft under willows. Tamerlane had been born a few miles to the south, and an afterglow of imperial patronage tinged the place. In later centuries it had enjoyed semi-independence from the emirate of Bukhara, and had flourished with more grace. Slavery was never allowed here. Even at executions, a traveller recalled, a criminal's throat would be mercifully cut before he was hanged.

Ruins still scattered it. The tomb of a son of Ulug Beg shone against the mountains, and a fifteenth-century congregational mosque survived in gutted dignity. Nobody guided or stopped me as I waded through poppies and cow-parsley into the wrecked mausoleum of Jehangir, Tamerlane's oldest and favourite son. Carved doors swung into a rank and sickly desolation, where only a slung canvas protected the grave against the pigeon droppings and bricks raining down from a disintegrating dome.

But the glory of Shakhrisabz, dwarfing all else, gleamed 47

in dereliction above its own parklands. Here the White Palace of Tamerlane had stood on the caravan-route to Khorasan and India, and had left behind a gateway so immense that nothing – not even the Bibi Khanum – could equal it. Such buildings were expressions of political power. The terror and grandeur of their appearance was crucial, for few ever entered them, and their gateways, like awesome warnings or advertisements, were huger, more portentous, than anything inside.

But I saw, as I approached this one, that it occupied a megalomaniac dimension of its own. It belonged among those dazing gargantuas of ruin – Karnak, Angkor, Baalbec – which might have been built by another species. Its central arch had long ago collapsed, but on either side a cylindrical tower merged into a nine-storeyed complex of buttresses and chambers, so that each jamb rose in a self-contained citadel 140 feet to a skyline of naked brick. The patina of tiles ripened as the entrance went deeper, edged in bands of peacock-blue, packed with white script. Exposed for centuries, they hung precariously in veins of cobalt and gold high up – an inexplicable delicacy of calligraphy and flowers.

The place was deserted except for a dreamy girl sitting on a ruined wall. She fell into conversation with the spontaneity of Turkic women when they feel unwatched. Tamerlane was definitely an Uzbek, she said, and from this I guessed her race. She walked naturally beside me. The ground was lightly paved inside the gate. High on either hand the piers were lanced by fissures and screamed with swallows, as if we were trekking through a canyon. Here the past was channelled to a narrow flood, and I sensed before us the limping tread of the monster over the grass-ringed stones, and the tramp of Shah Rukh after him, and of Ulug Beg and his patricidal son.

The girl talked with the childlike candour which perhaps only a stranger could release. She had the rosebud mouth and almond eyes beloved of Timurid miniatures, but already the flesh was loosening around them, and at twenty-nine her life was full of sadness. Her father had died young of a heart attack, and her brother too, at twenty-five. 'My mother still cries in the street.' The girl was the youngest in this decimated family, and felt in debt to them, as if she had somehow failed. 'I was accepted into university to study German without paying, because we were poor. My four sisters all got married, and helped me to live while I was there, since my stipend was so small.' She smiled sadly. Her mouth was already full of gold teeth. 'I had just two dresses, but they were enough.'

Beyond the gates we had entered a haunted void: a few brick foundations, some sunken steps and straggling trees. It was here that the Castilian envoy had been conducted in astonishment round a maze of reception halls, galleries and council chambers faienced in gilded blue, and saw under construction the banqueting-rooms where Tamerlane would feast with his princesses.

'It didn't matter having no money at university,' the girl went on. 'Everything was exciting then. I wore my hair down to here.' She trickled her fingers down her breast. Now she had a perm. 'What's hard is to love something, then find nobody wants it. And nobody much wants German.'

So in the end university had been a dazzling entrance to nothing, like the palace in which we walked. She stared hopelessly at the ground. 'I need to work, my husband earns so little. He's just a jeweller in crystal. We live in two rooms.' The unhappiness in this marriage needed no saying. 'I don't know what to do. I suppose I should start some business, but we've no money.'

'It should be easier to start a business now,' I said, but sounded cheerless even to myself. I seemed to be contracting her despair.

She shook her head. 'This isn't the West,' she answered. 'It will never be the West.'

She had seen American drama on television, and the West now appeared to her as delectable as it had once – under Moscow's censorship – seemed sordid. She looked at me with a faint, bovine hope and asked: 'How much do flights to Britain cost?'

I modified the price, but she sunk her head in resignation. I might have been talking of another cosmos. 'How much do apartments cost?' she inquired. 'How much is a refrigerator?' But now she was asking me not in aspiration but with the wan amazement of someone inquiring after another faith's paradise. Behind us the shattered palace had fallen from sight, and in front the streets of Shakhrisabz were closing in again.

A pang of childhood excitement surrounded the 'Veiled Prophet of Khorasan'. Perhaps I had read of him in Moore's *Lalla Rookh*, but more likely in the schoolboy vulgate of adventure stories and comic books. I have forgotten now. But the impossible romance, with its nimbus of messianic mystery, had remained obscurely with me, so that when I discovered that this phantasmal figure had died in the mountains around Shakhrisabz, I felt a tremor of boyish curiosity.

Even in history Muqanna, 'the Veiled One', is enigmatic, but from a conflation of old accounts – all of them hostile – he emerges as a sorcerer of seductive power, who raised the standard of revolt against the Arab conquerors of Central Asia in AD 776. At night he could summon up the moon from a deep well, it was said; and he covered his face with a golden mask, or a green veil, to spare men the effulgence of his countenance. Once a humble fuller at Merv, he proclaimed himself the ultimate incarnation of God, last and most sacred in the line which passed from Adam through Noah, Abraham, Moses, Jesus and Mahomet. He appears to have preached a blend of Persian Mazdeism and Islam, and promoted a primitive communism, even the sharing of wives.

His Arab foes ascribed his power to trickery. Deep in the well he refracted the rays of the sun in a great bowl of mercury, they said, and he covered his face because he was hideously deformed. He was one-eyed, bald, dwarf-like; he stammered. The claims and counter-claims only added to his mystique. But his white-robed followers raged across Transoxiana, subverting all ancient Sogdiana and the Bukhara oasis. The pagan Turks flocked to him, with a miasma of religious and political dissidents. They threatened to overwhelm the whole land. He himself crossed the Amu Dariya north into the heartland of his self-made faith, and for years defied the Arab armies from a fabled castle in the mountains near Shakhrisabz. Within its outer bastions spread orchards, a river, and cultivated fields, and high on a hill, in a massive keep, he lived alone with his harem and a single slave, a focus of scandal and awe.

But at last, in 786, a vast Arab army surrounded the walls. Thirty thousand of Muqanna's men deserted him, and opened the outer gates. Immured on the heights of the citadel, and realizing that his position was hopeless, he kindled a white-hot oven and incinerated all his possessions, even his animals. Then he commanded to follow him anyone seeking heaven, and with his family, harem and remaining followers, leapt into the furnace. When the insurgents entered the castle they found nothing at all, and at once the rumour started up that he had vanished into Paradise and would one day return.

The whereabouts of this castle obsessed me. In my empty hotel the tremolo of frogs kept me awake as they mated in the pool outside, and for half the night I pored over my large-scale maps of the region in search of a clue. But the Arab historians situated the castle only vaguely, close to Shakhrisabz on the heights of Sam, or Siyam, which was probably no more than a generic name for the northern Hisar mountains of today. My pen-tip dithered uselessly among the little villages. 'Zamas' raised a momentary hope, destroyed by its second-syllable stress. Tashkurgan – the ubiquitous Turkic word for a 'stone tower' – sent up a feeble promise. Otherwise, nothing.

For two days I bullied drivers to launch their derelict taxis along tracks and defiles in the neighbouring ranges. The late spring rains gushed and rustled through the clefts. The foothills bristled into counterfeit donjons and barbicans, which would disintegrate at our approach with the teasing monotony of mirages. In the Uzbek hamlets of mud and thatch, under roofs scarlet with wild-sown poppies, village elders shook their gnarled and fur-capped heads in ignorance of any vanished castle. One trip petered out at a pass where the driver refused to go on because of wolves. Another ended when a lorry skidded on a loose-stoned track and crashed into us. After some explosions of self-righteousness, the two drivers settled down to debate for an hour in a measured unravelling of pride. Then we limped home.

On the third day I found a tough, bad-tempered driver, so crippled that he was bound to his taxi like a centaur to its hooves. We moved east along a newborn river towards the village of Siyon (the name augured well) between terraces sprinkled with apple blossom. In front of us storm clouds rolled beneath the mountains, liberating their crests to float in solitude. The hills were all uncrowned; but sometimes their summits smoothed and spread like mesas, as if planed away for walls.

Suddenly, beyond Siyon, a mountain spur came thrusting into the valley. It reared up like a natural citadel. At its foot, where I imagined outer ramparts, the slopes were littered with crashed-down debris. Above, for some eighty feet, their scarps lifted sheer, fissured geometrically as if they were hewn blocks, before levelling out to a tatter of shrubs over the summit. It was impossible to tell which stones were carved, if any, and which natural. But the simulacrum was all of a mighty keep. It was hypnotic. Grey battle clouds were storming down the valley in collaboration, and had twined ornamentally along the upper bluffs. It was a forbidding and mysterious place, uninhabitable perhaps, I did not know.

I paid off the driver. It was only noon, and I reckoned on a three-hour climb. I marched across the intervening downland in reckless elation. Sapphire and cream flowers spiked the grass underfoot, and the spires of wild tulips gone to seed. I crossed two gullies heaped with black stones, like incinerated rivers, and scrambled up the crevice of a third. A four-foot snake erupted under my feet and flashed away through the tulips in a barbaric gleam of bronze. In front of me the castle (if that is what it was) rose ever more formidable. I strained to identify squared stones, but could not. In the silence an eagle rose and circled the summit on stiffened wings.

Many versions were told of Muqanna's end. It was said that before the Arab armies closed in, 50,000 of his subjects gathered beneath the castle and begged him to unveil his face to them. He prevaricated, warning them that the blaze of his countenance could kill them, but they insisted piteously, so he commanded them to return at sunrise. Just before dawn, he ordered his hundred-strong harem to line the parapets, while his followers waited below. As the sun rose, and his slave called on the people to behold the prophet's face, the odalisques canted their mirrors against the sunbeams and refracted them in a blinding conflagration of light. His followers hurled themselves on their faces in terror. Then, said the chroniclers, they took to Muqanna's cause with renewed zeal, and boasted that they had seen God.

This drama replayed itself easily on the clifftops in front of me. Labouring up a goat track through an airy dust of thistles, I left all doubts behind me. My reddened eyes swam with the past. I reached the saddle which joined the great spur frailly to the ranges behind it, and dropped exhausted on its rocks. I was pouring sweat. Around me russet butter-flies twitched and dark birds sang in the cliffs. I had no idea what I would find.

Some historians wrote that Muqanna's body was rescued from the furnace, and that its head was hacked off and sent to the caliph in Aleppo. But the starkest story was told long afterwards by a crone who claimed to be the last survivor of his harem. As the besiegers closed in, she said, the prophet feasted his women and ordered them to drain their goblets. But she sensed that the wine had been poisoned, and poured the drink unseen into her collar. As her companions died around her, she only feigned death. For a moment, she said, Muqanna surveyed the carnage, then she saw him go to his slave and strike off his head. Finally he removed his robe, and leapt into the furnace. 'I went over to that oven,' she said, 'and saw no trace of him. There was no one alive in the castle.'

Now, stumbling through the indigo flowers which swarmed across the summit, I could imagine a whole city here, or none. The porous rock had been split and polished into the sleekness of sculpture by millennia of exposure to the rain. I traversed it in a madness of indecision. It was impossible to be sure if the stones which balanced on top of one another had been laid by men or fragmented by wind, or if the runnels were those of water or chisel.

I struggled from natural terrace to terrace. Sometimes the storm-gouged outcrops seemed to have been slotted for posts and rafters. Dwarf oaks blurred every shape, with wild apricot trees wreathed in caterpillars. Once I came upon a plateau quartered and squared like a parquet floor. But it was a quilt of natural stone. In one place only, a vallum of boulders had been raised too regularly for chance, and I found traces of dissolved clay: a bandit's lair, perhaps.

At last I sat down bewildered on the cliff edge. Below me the valley made a vista fit for any reincarnate god. The threatened storm had gone, and the river threaded through mist in a silver torque, from which the far calls of goatherds ascended. All around, the slopes deluged with the white scented buds and violet pods of shrubs unknown to me, and I gave up wondering if I was seated on the ravaged castle, and listened, without history, to the river.

PENGUIN 60s

ISABEL ALLENDE · *Voices in My Ear*
NICHOLSON BAKER · *Playing Trombone*
LINDSEY BAREHAM · *The Little Book of Big Soups*
KAREN BLIXEN · *From the Ngong Hills*
DIRK BOGARDE · *Coming of Age*
ANTHONY BURGESS · *Childhood*
ANGELA CARTER · *Lizzie Borden*
CARLOS CASTANEDA · *The Sorcerer's Ring of Power*
ELIZABETH DAVID · *Peperonata and Other Italian Dishes*
RICHARD DAWKINS · *The Pocket Watchmaker*
GERALD DURRELL · *The Pageant of Fireflies*
RICHARD ELLMANN · *The Trial of Oscar Wilde*
EPICURUS · *Letter on Happiness*
MARIANNE FAITHFULL · *Year One*
KEITH FLOYD · *Hot and Spicy Floyd*
ALEXANDER FRATER · *Where the Dawn Comes Up Like Thunder*
ESTHER FREUD · *Meeting Bilal*
JOHN KENNETH GALBRAITH · *The Culture of Contentment*
ROB GRANT AND DOUG NAYLOR · *Scenes from the Dwarf*
ROBERT GRAVES · *The Gods of Olympus*
JANE GRIGSON · *Puddings*
SOPHIE GRIGSON · *From Sophie's Table*
KATHARINE HEPBURN · *Little Me*
SUSAN HILL · *The Badness Within Him*
ALAN HOLLINGHURST · *Adventures Underground*
BARRY HUMPHRIES · *Less is More Please*
HOWARD JACOBSON · *Expulsion from Paradise*
P. D. JAMES · *The Girl Who Loved Graveyards*
STEPHEN KING · *Umney's Last Case*
LAO TZU · *Tao Te Ching*
DAVID LEAVITT · *Chips Is Here*

PENGUIN 60s

LAURIE LEE · *To War in Spain*

PATRICK LEIGH FERMOR · *Loose as the Wind*

ELMORE LEONARD · *Trouble at Rindo's Station*

DAVID LODGE · *Surprised by Summer*

BERNARD MAC LAVERTY · *The Miraculous Candidate*

SHENA MACKAY · *Cloud-Cuckoo-Land*

NORMAN MAILER · *The Dressing Room*

PETER MAYLE · *Postcards from Summer*

JAN MORRIS · *Scenes from Havian Life*

BLAKE MORRISON · *Camp Cuba*

VLADIMIR NABOKOV · *Now Remember*

REDMOND O'HANLON · *A River in Borneo*

STEVEN PINKER · *Thinking in Tongues*

CRAIG RAINE · *Private View*

CLAUDIA RODEN · *Ful Medames and Other Vegetarian Dishes*

HELGE RUBINSTEIN · *Chocolate Parfait*

SIMON SCHAMA · *The Taking of the Bastille*

WILL SELF · *The Rock of Crack As Big As the Ritz*

MARK SHAND · *Elephant Tales*

NIGEL SLATER · *30-Minute Suppers*

RICK STEIN · *Fresh from the Sea*

LYTTON STRACHEY · *Florence Nightingale*

PAUL THEROUX · *Slow Trains to Simla*

COLIN THUBRON · *Samarkand*

MARK TULLY · *Beyond Purdah*

LAURENS VAN DER POST · *Merry Christmas, Mr Lawrence*

MARGARET VISSER · *More than Meets the Eye*

GAVIN YOUNG · *Something of Samoa*

and

Thirty Obituaries from Wisden · SELECTED BY MATTHEW ENGEL